Gardening on
Lime and Chalk

A Wisley Handbook

Gardening on Lime and Chalk

J. R. B. EVISON

Cassell

The Royal Horticultural Society

THE ROYAL HORTICULTURAL SOCIETY

Cassell Educational Limited
Villiers House, 41/47 Strand,
London WC2N 5JE
for the Royal Horticultural Society

First published 1981
Second edition 1985
Reprinted 1988
Third edition 1994

British Library Cataloguing in Publication Data
A catalogue record for this book is available from the British Library

ISBN 0–304–32074–9

Photographs by John Glover, Photos Horticultural and Peter Stiles

Phototypesetting by RGM Typesetting, Southport
Printed in Hong Kong by Wing King Tong Co. Ltd

Cover: One of the beauties of gardening on chalk and limestone is the massed
display of summer flowers possible with good cultivation.
  Photograph by John Glover
p.1: The pendulous flower heads of Wisteria sinensis appear in May or early June
and measure up to 1 ft (30 cm) long.
  Photograph by Peter Stiles
p.2: Robinia hispida, the rose acacia, is an eye-catching shrub for early summer.
Back cover: Euphorbia robbiae is good ground cover.
  Photographs by Photos Horticultural

Contents

Introduction

Gardening on limy soils is easy provided one accepts two straight-forward principles. These are that you cultivate your soil so that adequate supplies of food and moisture are available to your plants and that you make the right choice of plant to grow in your garden.

There are a few groups of plants such as heathers and azaleas which cannot be grown, and it is not difficult to understand the envy that chalk gardeners feel on walking in an acid-soiled garden in May and seeing the glories of the rhododendron at every turn. But let them return in summer and search for anything in flower, and unless the owner be unusually wise, they may well feel that the infinite and all-season variety available in their own garden has much to commend it. Comparison between those fine National Trust gardens at Hidcote Manor in the Cotswolds and at Sheffield Park on acid Sussex clay may well illustrate the point.

So be of good cheer and heed the simple rules which follow.

Opposite: The red border at Hidcote Manor, Gloucestershire
Below: *Cotoneaster* 'Cornubia' is covered with glistening red berries in autumn (see p. 48)

— Chalk and other Limy Gardens —

Nearly half our gardens are limy or have to use water from a limy source; this is not, I believe, a very widely appreciated fact, but a glance at the geological map (opposite) will show it to be true. Such soils are often called *alkaline*, and this is simply an adjective which, in a horticultural sense, means opposite to acid.

The largest areas of these soils are the chalklands typified by those softly-contoured rolling hills which we know somewhat illogically as downs; these are situated mainly in southern England, but there is a broad chalk band north of the Thames Valley stretching via the Chilterns to the coast of Norfolk. The carboniferous limestones are mainly found in Cumbria, Northumberland and the Mendips, and give rise to the Westmorland stone beloved by builders of rock gardens. The magnesium limestone belt lies in a narrow snake-like band running north and south from Durham down to Nottingham, whilst the Cotswold-type limestone (Jurassic oolite) starts in Dorset and Somerset, throws a broad swathe across the land towards the Wash and then runs northwards to the Yorkshire coast and Flamborough Head.

Minority alkaline soils include limy clays, marls, and that difficult soil, the limy sand.

Most gardeners will know whether or not they are on an alkaline soil; one way of telling is to look at the wild flowers and weeds which occur naturally in the soil. Some of those which occur on calcareous soils are traveller's joy (*Clematis vitalba*), whitebeam (*Sorbus aria*) and common dogwood (*Cornus sanguinea*), but they are mostly seen in the south of the country. Others which are more widespread include small scabious (*Scabiosa columbaria*) and hoary plantain (*Plantago media*).

In a new garden a soil analysis is a wise investment, as it is not easy for the gardener to be sure about the degree of alkalinity or how much free lime is present. Its cost may easily be recovered if you are guided to the most effective and economical procedures. Up-to-date information on firms offering a soil analysis service is available from The Royal Horticultural Society's Garden, Wisley, Woking, Surrey GU23 6QB. Such an analysis will set out the level of the main plant foods such as nitrogen, potash and phosphates and the lime content. Usually there is also a recommendation as to the fertilizer applications necessary to restore normal fertility.

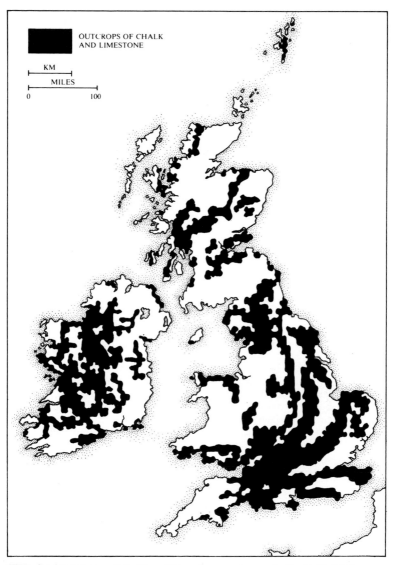

OUTCROPS OF CHALK
AND LIMESTONE

KM

MILES

0   100

Map showing areas of chalk and limestone outcrops in the British Isles.
(Based on data published by the Botanical Society of the British Isles in the
Atlas of the British Flora and reproduced with their kind permission)

The lime content will be shown as a number on the scale of pH
values. This is a logarithmic scale running from 1 to 14 and is
widely used as a measure of alkalinity or acidity in many fields.
Only the range 4 to 9 is applicable to soils, and it is the measure of
the soil solution.

9

If you prefer self-help, soil-testing kits (relating to pH only) can be purchased which have a reasonable degree of accuracy. A liquid is supplied which, when shaken with a sample of your soil, changes colour according to the acidity or alkalinity of the soil. The colour of this liquid is compared with the scale of colours on a chart provided enabling the pH and the soil condition to be read off. It is advisable to test a number of sites in a large garden. The following indicates the likely range:

Soil type	pH	Colour reaction
Alkaline	8.0–8.5	Blue-green
Slightly alkaline	7.5	Pale blue-green
Neutral	7.0	Green
Slightly acid	6.5–6.0	Yellow-green-yellow
Moderately acid	5.5	Orange
Very acid	5.0	Orange-red
Extremely acid	4.5	Red

Gardeners on alkaline soils are concerned with the scale above 7, which is neutral. It should not be forgotten that the scale is logarithmic, i.e., 8.1 is ten times as alkaline as 7.1. A soil pH greater than 8.6 is very rare but on the chalk downs 8.3 is not unusual.

Below: *Viburnum opulus*, the guelder rose, which also fruits very well in British gardens (see p. 48)
Opposite, above: *Clematis montana* 'Tetrarose', like the native clematis, thrives in chalky soils (see p. 50)
Opposite, below: *Hydrangea petiolaris* growing on a limestone wall (see p. 50)

CHALK AND OTHER ALKALINE SOILS

Chalk is soft pure limestone mainly derived from the skeletons and shells of minute marine creatures which lived and died in their myriads in the warm seas which once covered large parts of southern England. Thus was deposited a layer of natural calcium some hundreds of feet thick. Later ripples and contractions of the earth's crust threw this bed up into the well known rolling downs, the beauty of whose contours has no rival. Anyone gardening in these areas may well have six or seven hundred feet of chalk bed below them; this is of practical importance as it acts like a giant sponge rapidly absorbing rain and storing it in underground crevices. This gives surfaces which are so well drained that they may be cultivated just a few hours after heavy rain. This great boon to the gardener should not blind him to the fact that irreparable damage can be done to chalky soil structure by working it when very wet; if in doubt it is a good idea to work off a light plank.

A main variant in chalk is the size and number of flints. These are formed of fused silica and may weigh anything from an ounce to many pounds. Flints were used locally in the construction of buildings, walls and road foundations. In their 'knapped' form, i.e. split and squared, many a church tower is an object of great beauty. Observation of a chalk cliff face shows them to lie in layers often many feet apart. Their origin is uncertain; showers of meteorites and fossilized sponges are possible theories, but, in any case, most gardeners regard them as a major inconvenience to cultivation! The smaller ones at the surface make the drawing of drills for seed-sowing and hoeing difficult, whilst at a greater depth the thrust of a spade is so often diverted that in heavily flinted soils digging may best be done by fork.

The depth of soil over the chalk layer is critical, for the success of the garden depends on it. The gardener who finds 15 inches (40 cm) is lucky indeed; this will only be exceeded in valley bottoms and sometimes on the more level plateaux of the downs. On sloping land where erosion can take place 4 inches (10 cm) is quite common and this presents a major problem to the cultivator; indeed, he must bend his best efforts to increase its depth as described later.

The physical characteristics of the chalklands are that they are 'light' in the sense that they are easy to work; that they dry quickly and easily, needing no drainage system; and they are warm, i.e. they take up sun heat quickly when spring returns, which leads to early crops.

Against this one must recognise they are poor in plant foods:

they lack humus as organic matter and, when added, whether in peat or compost or any other form, it breaks down and disappears exceptionally quickly; when wet they are intolerant of pressure whether from foot or wheel, and may become sticky, intractable and lose their crumb structure for many months when maltreated in this way. A hard frost is the most effective remedy.

Cultivation of chalklands

It is widely accepted that the most effective method of combating the disadvantages outlined above is to ensure that the surface is regularly cultivated, in the right weather conditions, to a depth of two spits, i.e. two spades depth.

If you are fortunate enough to be working in a valley bottom with 18 inches (45 cm) of soil and subsoil, this is easily effected by the method of digging known as bastard trenching. This involves digging to the depth of two spades, leaving each spit at its original level and working compost into the lower spit.

However it is much more likely that 9 inches (23 cm) of soil with firm chalk beneath will be the problem. The essential difference is the treatment of the second or lower spit. Solid chalk or chalk with flints is unlikely to be capable of being broken up by spade or fork; a pick or mattock wielded with a full swing may be necessary. It is not essential that the lumps be broken up finely; once it is in rubble form most plant roots will cope with it and break it up further. Humus should be forked into this second spit, remembering that if you are to plant trees or shrubs or long-lived perennials, it is the only chance available to build up a store of potential food among the chalk rubble.

One cannot leave the cultivation of chalkland without a reference to a form of localised subsoil known at least on the South Downs as 'coombe rock'. An inaccurate description, for it certainly is not rock-like in density and it is not always found in valleys or coombes. It is an inhospitable mixture of marl and fine chalk debris which occurs in strata of varying thickness between the solid chalk and the top soil. It is grey-brown in colour; solid but brittle in texture; very alkaline – pH 8.6 and over – and useless for plant growth. Of course it is to be avoided if at all possible; if it has to be dealt with, excavation and removal has everything to be said for it save expense, and once dug out it makes a useful foundation for roads and paths. Should you have to cultivate it, treat it as an alien, break it up to about a spade depth and keep it open with rubble, flints or stones if available. It seems useless to add humus, which disappears in a few weeks. Do not mix soil or subsoil with it. Improve the upper layer as much as you can and leave the coombe rock to its own devices.

Above: *Pulsatilla vulgaris*, the Pasque flower, a plant which thrives on alkaline soils (see p. 29)
Below: *Arbutus unedo*, the strawberry tree (see p. 30)

Above: *Spirea* 'Anthony Waterer' (see p. 45)
Below: *Caryopteris* × *clandonensis*, one of the best late-flowering blue shrubs
(see p. 44)

Limy clays

These difficult soils appear in relatively small areas in many places such as the North and South Downs and East Anglia, where they occasionally overlay the chalk. There is also a thin, interrupted diagonal belt of lias clay running from the south-west towards the Wash.

A prime requirement for successful gardening on these soils is to ensure that surface water can run away, for natural seepage is unreliable and slow. Since water has very little inclination to move sideways in heavy soil, conventional drainage by tiles in a herring-bone fashion is rarely a success. Fortunately many alkaline clay soils are on sloping land. This good fortune, if allied to shallow slits or v-shaped trenches about 6 inches deep (15 cm) on the surface and filled with grit and very coarse sand, can provide much needed relief from excessive moisture. They need to lead to a deeper trench, ditch or other outfall.

Where none of these drainage practices can be employed, some gardeners have had success by planting shrubs and similar plants on shallow mounds so that the crown of the plant is 6 to 9 inches (15–23 cm) above general level, permitting them to survive periods of waterlogging conditions. For a year or two until a good root system has been built up, they need watering in very dry periods.

Limy clays are usually rich in plant food and wisely chosen plants will grow and flourish abundantly. On the reverse side of the coin they have all the faults of clay; slow to warm up in the spring, i.e. cold; heavy to cultivate and sticky when wet, turning bone-hard at the first hint of drought. The caution given about working chalk soils when wet applies with even more force here, for in bad conditions it is easy to destroy the surface structure. Indeed, just walking on the wet surface may cause such consolidation that these soils become unworkable when dry weather returns.

Gardening is a practical art and there are cultivation deadlines which it is necessary to keep, especially as spring approaches. Much can be done in open beds or borders or in the vegetable garden by working off boards or light planks. A number of small ones are usually used, as they often need to be moved with one hand to the next area. If making a garden on clay there is much to be said for many narrow paths from which borders can be tended. Recent attention has been directed towards growing vegetables on this type of bed system.

Limy clays benefit as do all alkaline soils from the addition of heavy dressings of humus in one of its many forms. Traditionally their structure was improved by adding burnt earth. Anyone who has made a bonfire on bare earth will be aware of the changed structure of the soil immediately beneath. It has become bone-dry and crumbly. This seems a permanent state and when dug in greatly improves even the stickiest clay.

Some years ago the then President of the Royal Horticultural Society who gardened on a most unfriendly clay, gave the following advice – 'Burn as much as possible of the clay. I get all the old tree stubs, roots, big bits of wood and everything similarly burnable in the winter and make an enormous fire and when there is great heat in it I put the clay right on top of the fire. I build it up into a cone and let it cook slowly. The fire will come through here and there after a day or so; as soon as it does the hole should be plugged up. In this way the fire can go on for three or four weeks, provided one stops up the holes every day; in the end there are several tons of beautifully burnt clay which is lovely stuff. it is like brick dust, it handles well, it digs in beautifully and even in its pure state the plants seem to revel in it.'

Smaller gardens can greatly benefit from a scaled-down version of the above, as burnt earth never regains its stickiness. Care should be taken, especially in the early stages, that smoke does not create a nuisance for neighbours. It is not an offence to burn garden refuse, even in a Smoke Control Area which refers only to smoke from domestic chimneys, but there may be a complaint from neighbours.

Similar physical improvements can be made by digging in ashes, sawdust, sweepings – indeed uncontaminated gritty material of any kind.

When digging clays, it is wise to do this as early as possible in the autumn, leaving a rough surface by angling each spit so as to expose a large surface area to the beneficial breaking up effect of frost. The heavier this frost is the better its action. By spring the soil should fork down into a very reasonable seed bed.

Limestone soils

Limestone is an extremely hard form of calcium carbonate. The alkalinity of the overlying soil tends to be less, with a pH value of around 7.5, than those associated with the chalklands where pH can be 8.0 and greater. Generally this is light, dries rapidly, and, in common with all limy soils, needs copious supplies of humus. Soil depth is generally greater than over chalk and sufficient for normal good garden practice. Given good cultivation and a wise selection of plants, very successful gardens can be created.

SOURCES OF HUMUS

It cannot be over-emphasised that adequate supplies of humus are the key to successful gardening on limy soils and the lighter the soils the truer this is. Bulky organic sources of humus are increasingly difficult to obtain. The following are the more important ways in which the immense appetite of alkaline soils for humus can be met.

Compost. Perhaps the best and certainly the cheapest way to supply humus comes from the garden's own resources, whose waste forms suitable material for a compost heap. These include weeds, soft prunings, non-greasy household vegetable peelings and scraps, autumn leaves, dahlia tops, pea and bean haulm and any other sappy garden waste available. Lawn mowings are best composted separately. It is advisable to exclude perennial weeds such as couch grass, convolvulus, ground elder, oxalis, etc., rose and other thick-stemmed hard prunings, and diseased plants. These are best burnt in such a way as not to annoy neighbours.

Make sure no plastic bags, tin foil, glass or tins are included. Cabbage and brussels sprout stalks are best smashed with a hammer to assist quick decay.

A compost heap is most easily made in layers about 12 inches deep (30 cm). Start with a base 5 to 7 feet (1.5–2 m) square in a secluded corner. Tread down, sprinkle with 1 oz (30 g) or more of sulphate of ammonia, and water. Continue to build up layer by layer to about 5 feet high (1.5 m). The vegetable matter is broken down by bacteria and other soil organisms which thrive best if given air, water, nitrogen (hence the sulphate of ammonia), a high temperature and non-acid conditions. The latter is of course natural to alkaline soils. Accelerators are available to use instead of sulphate of ammonia if desired. Decomposition is speeded up if the heap is turned after six weeks, moving the outside material to the centre in the process and watering any of the material that is dry. However, this 'turning' is not essential and even if not turned the heap should be like dark crumbly soil in a few months. Ready -made wooden or wire bins are available if appearance is important or space scarce.

Autumn leaves. The leaves of trees growing on alkaline soils, especially chalk, do not make good leaf mould. In this they are quite exceptional and it applies even to beech – normally one of the best for this purpose. Presumably the chemical composition derived from highly alkaline soil inhibits the normal process of decay. Of course they do ultimately break down but to a texture

The Oregon grape, *Mahonia aquifolium*, grows happily in shade (see p. 61)

best described as slimy; certainly it has no resemblance to those crumbly brown flakes once so beloved by the greenhouse gardener for his potting composts. Chalk gardeners are denied one of gardening's most useful aids. His autumn leaves need not be wasted; they are best either dug into trenches at leaf fall when winter digging, or added sparingly to the compost heap.

Bulk manures. Most practical gardeners give farmyard manure a high rating, not for its food content – which though nicely balanced is not high – but for the kindly way in which it breaks up to provide humus; soil rich in humus is usually very fertile. If the manure purchased from farm or stable is fresh, do not use until it has been stacked – if possible covered – until partly decomposed. The ammonia produced in the early stages of decay is not enjoyed by the plant roots. A layer 4 to 6 inches thick (10 to 15 cm) makes a satisfactory addition when dug in.

Town refuse. Some local authorities select suitable humus-based parts of their refuse collection and sell the pulverised product. It can contain up to 50% organic matter. Where available, especially on heavy soils, it is a cheap and effective method of soil improvement. The nutrient content is low. Other local authorities sell an

19

odourless product of sewage sludge. It is essential to get an assurance that no toxic metals likely to damage plants are present.

Wool shoddy. This by-product of the woollen industry is an excellent manure for those living near enough to a source of supply to buy economically. About 1 lb per square yard (0.56 kg/m²) will give a gradual supply of nitrogen over many months and also have a very good effect on soil structure.

Seaweed. Seaweed is another local source of humus. One of the oldest known manures, it has been used for centuries in coastal districts. It has a minor manurial value but the chief benefits are derived from its humus potential. Its main disadvantage is the extremely unpleasant odour it gives off when rotting. If dug in immediately this problem does not occur.

Spent mushroom compost. In some parts the residue of mushroom beds is given away for the cost of cartage; in others a small charge is made, often for the plastic bags containing a convenient quantity to put in the boot of a car. Add a compound fertilizer such as Growmore at 1½ lb per cubic yard (0.85 kg/m³) before digging in. It is less valuable in limy gardens in that chalk is often used to make up the compost for mushrooms so the garden's pH is only slightly lowered.

Green manuring. This is a method of growing one's own manure. A seed which produces abundant foliage rapidly is sown and the resultant crop is dug in a few weeks later, sometimes with 1 oz sulphate of ammonia per square yard (33g/m²) to assist in rapid decay. It needs an area vacant for at least eight to ten weeks, which makes it more suited to the vegetable garden or allotment. Quick maturing seeds like rape – often sold as mustard – can be sown in spring and dug in before planting winter green crops, or after early potatoes to be dug in during autumn or winter. Try to dig in when 4 to 6 inches high (10 to 15 cm), as digging is difficult when growth is taller. Clover and vetches are an excellent choice as, like peas and beans, they live in association with a bacteria which, living in nodules on the roots, has the ability to extract nitrogen from the air and fix, i.e. solidify, it in a root nodule. This nitrogen becomes available to the succeeding crop as the roots decay.

Other sources of humus are sometimes available if a keen eye is kept open. Building sites occasionally provide surplus soil which can be made available if good relations are established in the time-honoured way with the site foreman. Factories using natural materials may have a suitable waste product; saw mills may produce pulverised bark. Sewage farms which do not normally sell can be helpful if tactfully approached. Local initiative can be very productive.

THE LIME-HATERS

Botanists describe plants as *calcicoles* – the lime-lovers, or *calcifuges* – the lime-haters. Gardeners find it difficult to be so precise. It is true that on a train journey it may be possible to tell immediately the line leaves chalk or limestone by the cut-off of certain types of vegetation, for example, foxgloves and broom rarely grow on alkaline soils so their presence or absence is a good indicator. However, one cannot classify the foxglove as a lime-hater as when planted on limy soils – even chalky ones – it does very well and is typical of a number of plants which refuse to be strictly categorised.

This handbook is primarily concerned with those plants which do well on limy soils, but it may be helpful to look at the negative side first and list those plants which long experience has shown it is inadvisable to plant, as it is so rarely possible for them to grow freely and look happy on alkaline soils. Many are North American or Japanese in origin.

Chaenomeles × superba 'Crimson and Gold' (see p. 39)

*Plants disliking all alkaline
    soils*

(When the name of a genus,
    e.g. *Camellia*, is given, all
    species in it are included.)
Abies (except *A. cephalonica,
    A. pinsapo, A. × vilmorinii*)
Arctostaphylos
Calluna
Camellia
Cardiocrinum
Clethra
Corylopsis pauciflora
Crinodendron
*Cytisus multiflorus,
    C. scoparius*
Daboecia
Desfontainea
Embothrium
Enkianthus
Erica (except *E. × darleyensis,
    E. erigena, E. herbacea,
    E. terminalis*)
Eucryphia (except *E. cordifolia*)
Exochorda racemosa
Fothergilla
Gaultheria
Gentiana (except *G. acaulis,
    G. septemfida*)

Grevillea
Halesia
*Iris douglasiana, I. innominata,
    I. kaempferi*
Kalmia
Kirengeshoma
Leptospermum
*Lilium auratum, L. canadense,
    L. lancifolium, L. sargentiae,
    L. speciosum, L. superbum*
Lithospermum diffusum
Magnolia (except
    *M. grandiflora,
    M. × highdownensis,
    M. kobus, M. × loebneri*)
Meconopsis betonicifolia
Menziesia
Nothofagus
Nyssa
Pachysandra terminalis
Pernettya
Picea
Pieris
Quercua alba, Q. rubra
Rhododendron
Taxodium
Tsuga heterophylla
Vaccinium

TYPES OF CHLOROSIS AND THEIR TREATMENT

The term chlorosis denotes any yellowing of normally green tissues due to partial failure of the green pigment (chlorophyll) to develop. It can be due to many different troubles which are described below.

Weather damage. Cold-induced chlorosis is common in spring due to the green colour being absent from the parts of the plant that were making the most active growth when the cold spell set in. This trouble occurs frequently on young magnolia leaves which become very pale or almost white. Leaves so affected remain in this condition for the rest of the season and there is no treatment which can be carried out to restore the green colour to the foliage.

Waterlogging and weedkiller damage. Yellowing of leaves or parts of leaves can also occur as a result of waterlogged soil conditions; yews and narcissus being particularly susceptible to this type of injury. Misuse of weedkillers, notably para-quat/diquat mixtures, can also result in chlorotic patches or even complete yellowing of leaves. Plants or leaves affected in the latter way will again remain discoloured for the rest of the season, but when waterlogging is the cause of the trouble it may be possible to improve the condition of the plants by spraying them with a foliar feed.

Mineral deficiencies. Chlorosis due to the troubles described above usually shows as complete yellowing of leaves or scattered yellow blotches showing no particular pattern. However, by far the commonest cause of chlorosis is a lack of certain trace elements within the leaves because the plant roots have been unable to absorb them from the soil. In these circumstances the yellowing occurs between the veins of the leaves, often resulting in a V shaped pattern. Typically the veins of the young leaves stand out a darker green against a yellow background but when the disorder is severe all the young leaves appear entirely bleached.

In soils having a high pH (7.5 and over) both manganese and iron can be 'locked up' in the soil so that they become unavailable to plants. Often it is not possible to decide whether a lack of one or both elements has caused the symptoms.

However the chlorosis shown by many plants growing in chalky or limestone soils is due to iron alone being made unavailable to them and is described as 'lime induced'. Where the pH is 8.0 or above peaches, hydrangeas, ceanothus and chaenomeles are likely to show lime induced chlorosis. Sometimes the symptoms are so severe that the leaves are white. Young growths are always the most severely affected; scorching of the leaf margins and tips occurs in extreme cases. However in milder cases it may be difficult to distinguish between iron, manganese and magnesium deficiencies. It is not usually possible to solve the problem directly by applying iron compounds to chalky and limestone soil since the iron becomes 'locked up' very rapidly. Only if the element can be dissolved in the soil water can it be actively absorbed by the roots.

Treatment of lime-induced chlorosis

It may be possible to restore some of the green colour to the

23

foliage of plants showing lime-induced chlorosis by applying a special chemical formation of iron. Where the trouble occurs regularly every year however some effort should be made to prevent it. The addition of plenty of humus such as compost, leaf-mould or farmyard manure is recommended. The presence of actively decomposing organic matter in the soil decreases the possibility of iron deficiency, probably by increasing the carbon dioxide content of the soil thus lowering the pH in the vicinity of the plant roots. If the humus can be acidic e.g. crushed and chopped bracken or pulverised bark it will be even more beneficial.

Chemical treatments include soil application of chelated compound or fritted formulation of iron. They are sold under the name of Sequestrene or Sequestered Iron and may have added other trace elements commonly deficient on chalkland like manganese and magnesium. These are effective as they are capable of dissolving in the soil water and then being actively absorbed by roots. Thus leaves can resume their normal function; the effect can be spectacular but is unlikely to last more than a year. Treat claims that they enable rhododendrons and azaleas to grow freely in chalk with caution.

Foliar sprays of iron chelates are available. They work more rapidly but incur more time and trouble. Apply in dull conditions to the whole leaf surface on three or four occasions, allowing two weeks between sprayings.

It is not uncommon for chlorotic plants to appear in a particular part of a garden or even as an isolated plant in an otherwise healthy group, presumably because the pH in that area is singularly high. In such cases it may well be worthwhile trying to reduce the pH by systematically applying powdered sulphur at 4 oz per square yard ($130 \, g/m^2$) twice a year until testing of the plant's health indicates the required improvement. This is a biological process in which the powdered sulphur is oxidised to sulphuric acid by the soil bacteria. Since they work better when the soil is warm, it should be remembered that the process will be much slower in the winter months.

Aluminium sulphate and ferrous sulphate can also be used but are best applied to vacant ground. Apply either chemical at 4 oz per square yard ($130 \, g/m^2$). Rake in well and water in dry weather. Test for pH after two or three weeks and repeat if necessary.

Many years of experience of gardening on chalk and of the frailties and disappointments of chemical treatments have led me to a healthy respect for the usefulness of fritted trace elements. These contain a balanced amount of those elements of which a plant needs but little but whose absence is rapidly translated into ill-health as we have seen in the case of iron inducing chlorosis. These trace elements are iron, manganese, zinc, copper, boron and molybdenum. Fritted trace elements are slowly soluble over a long period and if applied when planting may prevent trouble occurring. Some fertilizers have fritted trace elements added.

It should always be remembered that to effect a cure by lowering the pH on chalk soil is never easy and always liable to be temporary. Therefore, when planting on these soils it is important to avoid those species especially liable to chlorosis. A list is appended of plants subject to chalkland chlorosis. I use this description as chlorosis becomes much more serious when the pH approaches 8.0 and above, which most frequently occurs on thin chalk.

Making a list of especially prone plants is complicated by the fact that plants in one genus do not always behave similarly in this respect. Taking the *Escallonia* as an example, of the thirty or so species and cultivars in commerce they are often referred to as large- or small-leaved according to whether their leaf size is greater or smaller than about one inch. All the large-leaved – and they include such good plants as 'Iveyi', a delightful white, and the crimson 'C.F. Ball' – grow happily on chalk. Most hybridising in the escallonias has been among the small-leaved and there lurks among the parents used a trouble-maker for those on chalky soil in the shape of *E. virgata*. This hails from Chile, is white, graceful and hardy, but an emphatic lime-hater. Unfortunately for those who garden on such soils it has passed on this lime intolerance to all its children. It is safest not to plant any of the small-leaved cultivars even though it means leaving out such excellent plants as 'Langleyensis', 'Edinensis', 'Slieve Donard' and many others; some with larger leaves like 'Donard Seedling', 'Donard Star' and 'Apple Blossom' have been known to succumb too.

Plants disliking shallow chalk soils

This list contains plants which are generally lime-tolerant but which are not satisfactory on shallow chalk soils, where they may be subject to chalkland chlorosis.

Acer japonicum, A. palmatum,
  A. rubrum
Castanea
Ceanothus caerulus, C. 'Gloire
  de Versailles', C. × pallidus
Chaenomeles
Cornus canadensis, C. florida,
  C. kousa, C. nuttallii
Daphne blagayana, D. mezereum

Elaeagnus
Escallonia bifida, E. virgata,
  small-leaved cultivars (see
  above)
Eucalyptus (except E. parvifolia)
Exochorda (except E. korolkowii)
Fabiana
Hydrangea macrophylla,
  H. serrata

Indigofera heterantha
Liquidambar
Lupinus (except *L. arboreus*)
Magnolia
Meconopsis (except *M. cambrica*)
Phlox paniculata
Pinus – all 5-needled species
Populus nigra, P. trichocarpa

Prunus laurocerasus
Quercus
Skimmia reevesiana
Spirea 'Anthony Waterer', *S. × billiardii, S. × brachybotrys, S. douglasii, S. japonica*
Stephanandra incisa
Weigela florida

FERTILIZERS

In contrast to animals, plants have the ability to make their own food. This is made in the green leaf using light as the energy source from absorbed nutrients. Principal among these are carbon, oxygen and hydrogen, obtained from the air and from soil water; from the latter source the elements most likely to be needed in large quantities – *Nitrogen* (N), *Potassium* (K_2O) and *Phosphorus* (P_2O_5) – are also obtained. The chemical symbols attached are those used on bags of fertilizer as a shorthand to indicate the contents. A percentage figure is added to indicate the concentration, i.e. sulphate of ammonia (20.8%N).

Escallonia 'Iveyi' makes a beautiful contribution in August (see p. 45)

Other elements likely to be needed in small quantities are discussed under *Chlorosis*. (p. 22).

Deficiencies in nitrogen, phosphorus and potassium are overcome by fertilizers which may be natural (organic) in origin, e.g. dried blood, or manufactured from chemicals (inorganic), e.g. sulphate of ammonia. Those generally available at the good horticultural sundriesman and suited to use by amateur gardeners on alkaline soils are:

NITROGEN (N) – Generally applied when leafy growth is required.

Inorganic	Sulphate of ammonia	20.8% N.
	Nitrate of soda	15.5% N.
Organic	Dried blood	14% N.
	Hoof and horn	13% N.

PHOSPHATES (P_2O_5) – Important for root growth.

Inorganic	Superphosphate of lime	16–18% P_2O_5
	Triple superphosphate of lime	46% P_2O_5
Organic	Bone meal	16–20% P_2O_5 4% N.
	Steamed bone flour	25–29% P_2O_5 1% N.

POTASH (K_2O) – Promotes even growth and flower/fruit/seed production.

Inorganic	Sulphate of potash	48.5% K_2O.
Organic	Wood ash	5–15% K_2O if kept dry.

The above are mainly single nutrient fertilizers. They can be, and often are, mixed to form a complete fertilizer. These may be formulated for a specific crop – tomato, rose, etc., and are well suited to that purpose. Frequently it is not necessary to particularise – a popular general fertilizer containing 7% of each main nutrient is 'Growmore'. Poultry manure is a natural source of nitrogen, best composted before use as it is concentrated.

I have tried to exclude from the above list those fertilizers which, because of their calcium content – as, for example sulphate of ammonia or Nitrochalk – tend to increase alkalinity. However, in the case of phosphates this cannot be done as there is no common phosphatic fertilizer which is not markedly alkaline. Therefore, use these nutrients only when really needed. Possibly poultry manure or hoof and horn might be used.

It is worth remembering that sulphate of ammonia, apart from being the quickest acting of the nitrogenous fertilizers, has the useful attribute on limy soils of removing its own weight of calcium in the course of becoming available to plants. Thus it assists in reducing alkalinity.

A SOIL PROBLEM

Choosing plants for alkaline soils has a major problem in that certain highly desirable plants refuse to grow in them. Examples are *Camellia*, *Rhododendron*, *Kalmia* and many ericas.

In view of the immense number of good plants which will flourish, the most sensible course is to accept the forbidden list and enjoy the remainder.

However, because it has a practical use in cultivating the garden, it may be worth examining a possible reason why some plants refuse to flourish in a limy soil. It may be the fact that there are a number of plants which lack the ability to absorb their food materials through the root hairs in the normal way. They depend on the presence of a soil fungus which coats their smallest roots with a layer of fine threads (mycelium); this by absorbing and passing on nutrients from soil water enables food to enter the host plant. In return the fungus receives food made by the plant's leaves. This state is known as symbiosis, i.e. associated existence, for the purpose of nutrition.

A number of plants live in similar social union – common examples are beech, oak, *Arbutus* and *Daphne*. It would seem that the particular fungus associated with the family Ericaceae, which includes the azaleas and rhododendrons, cannot thrive in alkaline soil water. Thus its host, having its food supply gravely diminished, languishes and dies.

Apart from the advisability on limy soils of not planting those kinds known to be affected in this way, it is wise when buying plants so affected to do so with a soil ball or in a container so that the required mycelium is already there to enable the plant to recover quickly from its move.

Where this is not possible, for example, when buying seedlings for a beech hedge, and if it is to go where no beech has been grown recently, then a few handfuls of soil obtained from near the roots of an established beech scattered along the trench when planting will encourage rapid and successful growth.

— Choosing Herbaceous Plants —

Perhaps because of their generally shallow rooting systems, compared with trees and shrubs, most herbaceous plants· are perfectly happy on chalk and lime; for that reason I shall mention them only briefly!

There are several good books on herbaceous plants available, amongst them *Perennial Garden Plants*, by Graham Stuart Thomas (Dent) and *Herbaceous Plants* by Kenneth Beckett (Croom Helm). These specialist books cover the subject in detail, so it is only necessary here to deal with the very few herbaceous perennials which will fail on chalk or lime. It is a very short list of which the lupin (with the exception of *Lupinus arboreus*, the tree lupin) is the most noteworthy. It is a great pity as it deprives the garden of one of the most colourful of herbaceous plants and foliage which contrasts excellently with other plants. *Meconopsis*, too, dislike very alkaline soils. The blue species such as *M. betonicifolia*, may grow reasonably but the flowers are an unattractive muddy blue rather than the kingfisher blue of the same plant on acid soils. Here again there is an exception – *M.cambrica*, the Welsh poppy, is happy enough to grow and make a nuisance of itself, seedlings appearing unbidden in all the wrong places (see p. 57). *Kirengeshoma palmata* will grow but looks so abnormal as to be an embarrassment. Certain *Iris* are calcifuge, notably *Iris kaempferi* from Japan and some Northern American species such as *I. innominata* and *I. douglasiana*. To these we should add the autumn-flowering gentians such as *Gentiana sino-ornata* and *G. farreri* and their hybrids and cultivars. A few plants are best avoided, not because they are intolerant of alkaline conditions but because it is rare that sufficiently moist soil can be provided. Among these are the many primulas such as the Candelabra group like *P. japonica* with *P. florindae* and *P. helodoxa*. I do not think that *Phlox paniculata* can be called calcifuge, although it is often written about as if it was. I know of many brilliantly successful clumps on alkaline or even chalky soils, but I suspect these are usually areas where the soil is well supplied with humus and unlikely to dry out rapidly.

One plant which deserves a mention as it is a native which thrives on chalk, is *Pulsatilla vulgaris*, the pasque flower (see p. 14).

Choosing Trees

Since the tree is the plant whose size will most dominate your garden, its choice is more than ordinarily important. It needs more consideration than the guide notes included in this Handbook, and I would refer you to another title in this series – *Trees for Small Gardens*.

There are a few trees which will tolerate a mildly alkaline soil but which are so unlikely to succeed on thin chalky soils that they are best avoided. These include all magnolias, *Styrax japonica*, *Photinia villosa* and all *Eucalyptus*.

Some trees which would succeed on a heavy alkaline soil include *Malus sargentii*, the smallest-growing crab apple with white, golden-anthered flowers in spring and small, bright red cherry-like fruits in the autumn; *Pyrus calleryana* 'Chanticleer', a pear of pyramidal outline with masses of pure white flowers and good autumn colour; *Sorbus* 'Joseph Rock', a mountain ash with especially attractive rich autumn colour as a setting for its amber-yellow fruits; and as a conifer, *Juniperus virginiana* 'Sky Rocket', a slim blue-grey finger pointing heavenwards.

On dry chalk, I would recommend *Arbutus unedo*, the Killarney strawberry tree (see p. 14), which bears its lily-of-the-valley-like flowers and circular red fruits at the same time in the autumn (I suppose the fruits have a vague strawberry appearance, but no amount of sugar and cream will make them edible); *Cotoneaster* 'Cornubia', with masses of bright red autumn fruits; and *Prunus subhirtella* 'Autumnalis Rosea', whose small pink flowers cheer the passer-by from October to March.

I do not think anyone is likely to regret planting any from the above short, short list.

The Shrub Garden through the Year

If trees form the most dominant feature of a garden, there can be no doubt that it is shrubs which provide the backcloth, the tapestry against which the garden is set and are thus of the utmost importance. From them you can have flower any day of the year; acquire foliage of infinite variety in colour, shape, size and texture; enjoy autumn tints, magnificent berries, brilliant and beautiful barks and shapes which range from the pencil to the Christmas pudding.

Let us take a walk around the garden season by season and identify what my experience leads me to believe are among the best of the best.

EARLY WINTER: NOVEMBER–DECEMBER

November and December may appear dull months but they need not be. It is the season when a number of very fine shrubs flower. *Mahonia japonica* is one of the most ornamental of all shrubs. It bears magnificent pinnate holly-shaped leaves each 1½ foot long (45 cm), deep green and gracefully pendulous, which make it an object of beauty the year round. At this season come the flowers; springing from the tip of each shoot are a number of pendulous racemes of lemon yellow, lily-of-the-valley scented flowers. There may be up to a hundred in a single chain and a thousand in the cluster. It is a tough character and grows well in the shade of trees. Another superb scent arises from *Viburnum farreri*. It is a thick deciduous bush; no sooner has it dropped its leaves than the young buds, which are pale pink, start to open into pure white clusters a couple of inches across. It used to be called *V. fragrans* and well deserved its title. At this time, too, we see the first flowers of the winter jasmine, *Jasminum nudiflorum* (see p. 34). Its striking bright yellow flowers clothe young green shoots from this season through to March in such profusion that a sprig or two can always be spared for a vase indoors. The largish garden should certainly have *Arbutus × andrachnoides*, one of the strawberry trees. In spite of having a Grecian species as father, it is quite hardy, flowering freely at this season bearing clusters of pitcher-shaped white flowers to be followed much later by round straw-berry-coloured fruits. Not least of its attractions is its remarkable cinnamon-red trunk and branches; few who have seen it in a shaft of winter sunlight can resist trying it (see p. 34).

   Bark can be as effective as flower in midwinter. The birches and snake bark and paper bark maples are excellent, but belong to the small tree section; some of the dogwoods and willows have startlingly brilliant young stems. *Cornus alba* 'Sibirica' is bright red, and *C. stolonifera* 'Flaviramea' is yellow. *Salix alba* 'Britzensis' has brilliant orange scarlet and *S. alba* 'Vitellina' has yellow stems. All must be cut back hard in spring as only one-year shoots have really good colour.
   Nearly all the family Ericaceae are lime-haters but a few ericas will grow well on alkaline soils, although not on thin shallow chalk for which they are not advised. *Erica carnea* is a

Prunus subhirtella 'Autumnalis Rosea', an excellent small tree for dry chalk

dwarf shrub which makes excellent shrubby ground cover. Its many cultivars span November to March or April. 'Eileen Porter' – rich carmine – starts in November (see p. 35) followed soon after by 'King George' – rose pink – at which the succession spills over into January where we will follow them.

LATE WINTER: JANUARY–FEBRUARY

The bleak months of January and February often contain the year's worst weather, but a number of plants take no notice of this and choose to brighten our day whenever we pass by. Many more cultivars of *Erica carnea* appear after Christmas. Have a look at a collection in flower before making a choice if you can. I would not miss 'Springwood White'; 'Vivellii', a deep carmine with bronzy winter foliage; or 'Springwood Pink'. Late cultivars like 'Ruby Glow' spill over into the early spring section amongst which I would try to include 'Aurea', whose deep pink flowers are followed by striking bright gold foliage in spring and early summer. No planting of ericas should be without *E.* × *darleyensis*, whose lilac-pink flowers span the whole winter. It is taller, about 3 feet (90 cm) and makes a break from the flatness of *E. carnea*. So also do those other lime-tolerant species, the rose-red *E. erigena* and the Corsican heath, *E. terminalis*, whose flowers are deep pink and whose branches are upright rather than spreading. Junipers associate well with ericas and being native to the chalk-lands do well in alkaline conditions. *Juniperus communis* 'Compressa' has a dwarf columnar shape which contrasts well with ground-hugging ericas as also does the larger *J. communis* 'Hibernica', the Irish juniper. Both are silvery green

  Chimonanthus praecox, the wintersweet, is not a plant for the impatient. It may well be five or six years before it rewards you with one of the garden's great scents. This is what you plant it for, as it has no claims to being a handsome bush or bearing flowers of startling effect. They are a waxy yellow with a purple heart. Much more noticeable are those of *C. praecox* 'Luteus', which are clear yellow, appear in February rather than January, but have markedly less fragrance. Either are best planted against a wall with flowering shoots spurred back like a fruit tree. This not only promotes young shoots upon which flowers are borne but it makes them flower earlier (see p. 38).

  The Cornelian cherry, *Cornus mas*, is a most cheerful February flowerer. It bears a multitude of tiny yellow flowers on the naked branches in a fluffy mist. In summer it bears the bright cherry red rose-hip size edible berries which give rise to its common name. 'Variegata' is an outstanding variegated form and there is also a golden form. These do very well on chalk but do not let success with this plant lead ycu to try some of the North American dogwoods like *C. florida*. They are definite calcifuges. Among the first of its family *Daphne odora* comes into flower this month; a small shrub with pinky white sweetly scented flowers which appreciates the shelter of a wall. I know of no daphne which refuses to grow on lime but quite a few which resent poor drainage – a point to watch when planting.

Below: *Arbutus × andrachnoides* growing in the chalk garden at Highdown, near Worthing, West Sussex (see p. 32)
Opposite, above: *Erica carnea* 'Eileen Porter' bears flowers from November onwards (see p. 33)
Opposite, below: *Jasminum nudiflorum* (see p. 32)

EARLY SPRING: MARCH–APRIL

Spirits rise with the lengthening days and nothing typifies this more than the mezereon, *Daphne mezereum*, well loved for centuries in the gardens from cottage to castle. It is an upright growing plant whose branches are covered with fragrant red-purple flowers to be followed by poisonous red berries. There is also a white-flowered cultivar 'Alba' with translucent yellow berries whose flowers are said to be even more strongly scented.

There is no doubt about the ability of the flowering currant, *Ribes sanguineum*, to grow and flower well in the chalkiest of soils. Doubts as to its worthiness for a place arise from its uninteresting appearance except when in flower. At that moment it is as valuable as it is popular. It bears a multitude of pendulous racemes from mid-March onwards. There are a number of cultivars ranging in flower colour from white to deep red. I think it is important to grow the deepest red you can as it is a most useful shrub to cut and encourage into earlier flower in a green-house; a most striking decoration in a sunny room. They do tend to fade somewhat under such care so the paler colours may appear anaemic. Good cultivars are 'Splendens', 'Pulborough Scarlet' and 'King Edward VII'. Perhaps the decision whether to plant or not depends on the size of one's garden. In very small gardens doubtless better use can be made of the space.

The tassel bush, *Garrya elliptica*, merits a place for its catkins which are among the most spectacular the garden has to offer. It is a light greeny grey evergreen and is best placed on a sunny sheltered bank or against a wall. There it will provide interest the winter long, first with its long suede-grey catkins which at the first surge of spring grow to some 8 inches in length (20 cm). Then the soft grey scales lift to reveal band after band of frilly stamens. The male is the best form. Do not be tempted to cut it for a flower arrangement unless you are content to cope with the continuous cascade of pollen which will be dropped; or cut shoots several weeks before the flowering period, strip the leaves and allow the catkins to develop in a greenhouse or sunny room. No pollen is then dropped (see p. 38).

This is of course the season of the forsythias, too well known to need any recommendation. If the numerous choices of species and cultivars are bewildering, try *Forsythia intermedia* 'Lynwood'; it is spectacular and makes a good garden plant.

Osmanthus delavayi is a 5 feet (1.5 m) evergreen of real quality. In late March it is covered with small ivory white, deliciously fragrant, tubular bells which contrast well with the small deep green leaves. One of its children, *Osmanthus × burkwoodii*, is a very handsome plant of great vigour. It has larger but equally sweetly-scented flowers and can be used as a hedge; it also makes a fine specimen plant. Either plant can be lightly clipped, when they flower even more freely.

Osmanthus delavayi, one of the most valuable shrubs for early spring

37

Opposite, above: *Chimonanthus praecox* 'Luteus', the fragrant wintersweet (see p. 33)
Opposite, below: *Garrya elliptica*, the tassel bush (see p. 36)
Above: The well-known *Kerria japonica* 'Pleniflora' (see p. 54)

The Japanese quinces, known and loved in our gardens for a couple of centuries as "Japonica", cannot be omitted in spite of a tendency to chlorosis on the most chalky soils. Hopefully the generic name is now settled as *Chaenomeles*, and under that name can be found a good range of beautiful and easily cultivated plants. *Chaenomeles speciosa* 'Nivalis' is white; 'Simonii' is dwarfer and its deep scarlet flowers exceptionally fine. *Chaenomeles × superba* 'Crimson and Gold' (see p. 21) has deep red petals and golden anthers; 'Knaphill Scarlet' is salmon-scarlet. 'Rowallane' has flowers of bright crimson which can be $1\frac{1}{2}$ inches across (4 cm). Its habit allows it to be trained easily against a wall. In such places it is wise, especially on chalk, to take great care in site preparation for builder's mortar added to an already alkaline soil is not a desirable combination. Good soil at planting and water in dry spells are the best insurance against chlorosis.

Towards the end of April come two of the best of all evergreen shrubs both about 6 feet high (1.8 m). *Berberis darwinii* comes from South America where it was discovered by Charles Darwin on his journey in the Beagle in 1835. It bears clusters of golden-orange flowers made more attractive by the red-gold sheen they bear before opening. The leaves are like a small three-pointed holly leaf, shining and dark green. A more graceful plant is *B. × stenophylla*. Left unpruned it produces long arching branches on which are borne a multitude of rich yellow flowers. It is one of the best plants for an informal hedge, and is quite happy on thin chalk but less vigorous.

LATE SPRING: MAY–JUNE

The high season for shrubs occurs in May and June. Since everything other than the forbidden list will grow, it is inevitable that many very suitable and worthwhile shrubs are omitted in this selection. This may be no bad thing, for there is a temptation to over-plant for this season from the abundance of small trees like the cherries, almonds, plums and peaches – to say nothing of the shrubs – with the result that the spread of flower in the garden becomes unbalanced.

No shrubs are happier on limy soils than the lilacs. You can divide them roughly into the common lilacs, which are familiar in most gardens, and the species. There are over three hundred cultivars in the country and about fifty can be bought in the trade. The 'best' is a personal judgement, but for me it might be *Syringa* 'Madame Lemoine' – double white; 'Madame A. Buchner' – rose-mauve, or 'Katherine Havemayer' – deep purple lavender. I would really like to direct your attention away from the common lilacs to the species. They have a more attractive habit as a rule, many fit better into the smaller garden and they bear at least as much flower. *Syringa velutina*, the Korean lilac, is a naturally small bush; it will take many years to reach its maximum of 5 or 6 feet (1.5 or 1.8 m), and bears its profusion of lilac-pink flowers even on small plants less than 1 feet (30 cm) high.

Syringa microphylla 'Superba', sometimes called the littleleaf lilac, is another slender charmer which throws its erect panicles of rosy pink flowers up at this season, has a little rest and then flowers again in September with the odd flower up to Christmas. The Rouen lilac, *S. × chinensis*, forms a medium-sized bush on which drooping panicles of fragrant lavender-pink flowers are borne. There is an excellent darker form, *Syringa × chinensis* 'Saugeana' which has reddish purple flowers. For sheer exuberance of flower I doubt if two children of *S. henryi* can be surpassed. One, *Syringa* 'Floreal' is an elegant shrub rendered invisible by its lavender-mauve flowers in early June, and *Syringa* 'Prairial', somewhat similar but with lavender-blue flowers.

The mock oranges or *Philadelphus* are delightful shrubs with showy, mostly white flowers, very sweetly scented. A number have the Award of Garden Merit; of these I rate *P.* 'Beauclerk' very highly. It starts to flower at the end of June with huge 2½ inch blossoms (6 cm) each with a rosy cerise zone in its heart. Unlike some others it has a graceful arching habit (see p. 42). If you want to reduce its size, cut out flowering wood immediately after flowering, rather as for raspberries, and encourage the young pale shoots which will be forming at the base. The plant will then settle down at about 3 feet (0.9 m) in height.

Flowering at the same time are the deutzias. There are beautiful white forms, but rather than compete with the mock oranges, it may be wise to choose from those two excellent pink hybrids, *Deutzia × elegantissima* which has an upright habit and late in June bears a multitude of clusters of fragrant rose-tinted flowers; or *D.* 'Mont Rose', on whose 6 feet arching stems (1.8 m) are borne its clusters of deepening rose-pink flowers which can become paler as they age (see p. 42).

Not all the genistas and cytisus are happy on chalk, but among those which are we have *Genista cinerea*, which cheers the garden in June with its masses of golden yellow flowers and the Moroccan broom, *Cytisus battandieri* (see p. 43). A large silvery grey shrub due to the mass of silken hairs which cover each leaf and young shoot, it welcomes a wall in cold gardens, but can also be grown in the open. The flowers are borne at the end of shoots and can be 6 inches long (15 cm) crowded with short-stalked golden yellow flowers. It is strongly scented with more than a hint of fruit. Some say fruit salad, some pineapple, but it is unusual and it is pleasant.

Blue is not a colour commonly found among shrubs, which renders *Ceanothus* most welcome. They are of Californian origin, which makes the hardiness of many suspect. One of the very best is 'Delight', worthy indeed of its name. It is one of the hardiest, but in cold exposed gardens it should have a sheltered spot where it will make a bush 10 feet (3 m) high. The glossy evergreen leaves darken as they mature and in May the panicles of rich blue flowers appear at the end of shoots and in leaf axils to form a magnificent blue cloud.

One of the most successful evergreens on chalk is the Mexican orange blossom, *Choisya ternata*. Its mass of white scented flowers show up well against the bright green leaves which are aromatic when crushed; it makes a hardy bush 4 to 5 feet high (1.2–1.5 m) and is equally happy in sun or shade (see p. 21).

Robinia hispida – the rose acacia – is one of those plants which visitors always stop at. It has large deep rose flowers, especially in its larger form, 'Macrophylla' which suggests a wisteria (see p. 2).

41

Opposite, above: *Philadelphus* 'Beauclerk', one of the best mock oranges (see p. 41)
Opposite, below: *Deutzia × elegantissima* 'Rosealind', with deep carmine-pink blossom
Above: *Cytisus battandieri*, the Moroccan broom (see p. 41)

SUMMER: JULY–AUGUST

Roses are the supreme universal favourites at their best in July. I have seen it written that roses do not like alkaline soils, especially chalk, but this is not my experience. Subject to the ground being properly prepared (see p. 13 onwards), I know of no rose which will not grow well, so your choice is as wide as the catalogue you use. What you must not expect is colour as intense as that achieved on heavy, slightly acid land, which is probably the best rose soil. So, provided you remember that the need for food and water on light land is greater than on heavier soils, you may plant roses freely.

At the other end of the scale and demanding no attention at all, is *Buddleja davidii*, perfectly happy in the poorest of soils, as witnessed by their colonisation of waste land such as bomb sites in London in the 1940/50s. Those who saw plants on these sites may remember that their colours left much to be desired, so the choice of good cultivars is important. Among the best are 'Royal Red' – reddish purple; 'Black Night' – the darkest purple, and 'Empire Blue' – deep blue.

Ceanothus, most of which are spring-flowering have already been mentioned, but *Ceanothus* 'Autumnal Blue' is one not to be missed. It is probably the hardiest of the evergreen *Ceanothus* and bears large panicles of rich blue flowers. If you have a garden where frost and cold are a special hazard, you may like to try C. 'Gloire de Versailles'. You can grow it as a large rounded deciduous bush which will give you large clusters of rich blue flowers from July until the frosts come. Even if it is cut down by frost it will break again from the base. Thin the bush lightly in April or grow it like a herbaceous plant and cut to the ground annually; mulch liberally if you do the latter.

Lavatera olbia, the tree mallow, is another undemanding plant which will grow to 5 feet (1.5 m) in one season. It carries its mallow-pink cups for month after month with the solitary demand that it be replaced every fourth year (see p. 47).

No garden should be without *Hypericum* 'Hidcote'; this very beautiful, almost evergreen 3 to 4 feet (0.9–1.2 m) shrub is in almost continuous flower from July to September. The flowers are cup-shaped and rich golden yellow which at a couple of inches across are the largest of any hardy hypericum. To keep it within bounds, prune back to 2 feet (60 cm) in spring (see p. 46).

Abelia × grandiflora has graceful arching branches bearing brilliant green foliage and from July to September clusters of pale pink and white bell-shaped flowers about $\frac{3}{4}$ inches long (2 cm). A good specimen may be 6 feet high (1.8 m).

Caryopteris × clandonensis is one of the best short late-flowering blue shrubs. If pruned well back each spring it results in a blue cloud about 1½ feet high (45 cm) in August and September (see p. 15). Although it is sometimes called the "blue spiraea", it is not in anyway related to spiraeas.

All species of hydrangea are suitable for mildly alkaline soils but *Hydrangea macrophylla* and *H. serrata* and their cultivars should be avoided on chalk and high pH soils because of their liability to become chlorotic. If you wish to grow hydrangeas – which will be some shade of pink on alkaline soils – they need shade, moisture and plenty of humus in the soil.

Another excellent hydrangea is H. *villosa* which is of the lacecap type; these produce their flowers in a flattened terminal head, an outer ring of infertile but very showy ray florets surrounding usually lighter coloured and less attractive, female flowers. This species has a central disc of small blue florets and an outer ring that is ruby-lilac. *Hydrangea paniculata* 'Grandiflora' must be one of the most spectacular of all the larger shrubs flowering in summer. Fully grown it may be 12 to 15 feet high (3.6–4.5 m) with each terminal growth a creamy white plume. A smaller earlier cultivar 'Praecox' flowers in July and is perhaps more suited to small gardens than the much bigger 'Grandiflora'.

Few people like to be without lavender, one of our best-loved shrubs. It provides soft grey foliage, blue or purple flowers, flower-heads which, when dried, provide a delightful long-lasting aroma, and tolerance to clipping for a short internal dividing hedge. *Lavandula* 'Hidcote' is an excellent 2 foot high (60 cm), deep violet-purple flowered cultivar (see p. 46).

The shrubby cinquefoils are amongst the most useful and trouble-free of garden shrubs. These potentillas are dwarf shrubs which flower continuously through the summer, are dense enough to smother weeds, accept any soil and have no troublesome pests or diseases. *Potentilla* 'Elizabeth' rarely reaches 3 feet (90 cm) and is spangled with rich soft yellow flowers; it is excellent to top a low wall. *Potentilla* 'Beesii' is worth growing for its silvery foliage alone, but it also bears attractive golden flowers.

Spiraea japonica 'Anthony Waterer' (see p. 15) is a valuable low-growing shrub which can be kept less than 3 feet (90 cm) by pruning hard back in spring each year. It then throws up shoots, each crowned with a broad, flat, rich crimson panicle of flowers; the shoots are occasionally variegated with pink and cream.

The cistuses are excellent on alkaline soils, although none are reliably hardy. Probably the hardiest is *Cistus* 'Silver Pink', a well named hybrid which makes attractive hummocks about 3 feet (90 cm) high. Its long clusters of pastel-shaded flowers look best against a dark background.

Warning to avoid the small-leaved escallonias has already been given, but there is no need to avoid that marvellous white-flowered evergreen *Escallonia* 'Iveyi'. Its handsome glossy leaves make a superb background for the large crowded panicles of white flowers. It has no peer in the August shrub border (see p. 26).

Opposite, above: *Hypericum* 'Hidcote', a very popular shrub (see p. 44)
Opposite, below: *Lavandula* 'Hidcote', one of the best lavenders (see p. 45)
Above: *Lavatera olbia* 'Rosea', the tree mallow (see p. 44)

AUTUMN: SEPTEMBER–OCTOBER

Essentially the season of berries and coloured foliage, this season
can rival any for sheer flamboyance. Unfortunately a substantial
number of the best leaf colouring autumn shrubs are denied to
those on high pH soils. The Japanese maples, like many plants
from that country, whilst not refusing to grow, do not flourish;
nor will *Amelanchier*, *Aronia*, *Enkianthus*, *Fothergilla*, *Nyssa*,
Hamamelis or *Vaccinium*, but amongst those which will thrive is
Berberis thunbergii – indeed a plant for all seasons. A bush about 3
feet in height (90 cm) its pleasant yellow spring flowers become
bright red berries in the autumn, and its leaves turn brilliant
scarlet with a hint of gold. *Berberis wilsonii* is a pleasing small
shrub of spreading habit with small soft green leaves which in
autumn turn to orange and red contrasting admirably with its
coral berries. Most people would be happy to have the smoke
bush or Venetian sumach, *Cotinus coggygria*, in their gardens for

its summer beauty even if it did not provide superb orange red autumnal foliage; this is especially so in the form 'Flame'. I would not suggest you plant the stags horn sumach, *Rhus typhina*, or its more refined cultivar 'Laciniata' unless you have a wild corner where it can be left to its own devices, or you are prepared for a running battle with the suckers with which it will try to dominate. If you have a place for it, then its pinnate leaves – like a giant ash – will bring a fern-like appearance to the shrubbery and autumnal colouring in red and orange and yellow.

If one had to choose the single plant whose autumn tints had made the widest impact, then it might well be the Boston ivy, *Parthenocissus tricuspidata* 'Veitchii', for there is scarcely a town or village where one cannot see it turning a very ordinary wall into a sheet of crimson with the arrival of autumn. It is widely miscalled Virginia creeper – a title which properly belongs to *P. quinquefolia* – no mean climber itself, and its five-lobed leaves also turn scarlet in October.

Berries also make a major impact at this season. Very few of these fail on alkaline soils. I would always try to find room for that excellent native plant the guelder rose, *Viburnum opulus*. Its flattened white heads of flower brighten the summer months and are followed by bunches of striking translucent red berries in great abundance, which often remain far into the winter (see p. 10). Its green maple-like leaves assume brilliant autumn tints.

Cotoneaster contains some of the most beautiful of the berried shrubs and they do not seem to mind even thin chalk if it is properly prepared. Among the most spectacular is *Cotoneaster* 'Cornubia'. It is a 12 foot (3.6 m) semi-evergreen whose branches form arching sprays which by late September are weighed down with abundant bunches of bright red fruit (see p. 7). Other large semi-evergreens of outstanding merit include *C.* × *watereri* and the many named clones which may have salmon-pink or yellow or orange-red fruits in addition to the brilliant red of the type. Among the yellow-fruited cotoneasters *C.* 'Exburiensis' may be the best. At the dwarfer end of the cotoneaster choice – there must be at least a hundred in commerce – is the "fishbone cotoneaster", *C. horizontalis*, which looks best if trained hard against even a north or eastern wall and there gives a rich harvest of fruit and autumnal leaf. Perhaps it has been rather over-planted. This is not true of that best of bank scramblers, *C.* 'Decorus'. The ¼ inch diameter (0.5 cm) brilliant scarlet berries colour up in September and October and as they do not seem to be a favourite with the birds may still be there in February. It does well on chalk and seems to enjoy full sun.

It is doubtful if there is any shrub which revels in alkaline conditions, even thin chalk, more than *Euonymus* or the spindle-berries as their deciduous forms are known. *Euonymus europaeus* is a native and a familiar part of the hedgerows on the chalk. It has given rise to a number of forms of which 'Red Cascade' has the Award of Garden Merit; it has brilliant autumn foliage and can produce such a heavy crop of rose red fruits that its naturally arching branches are weighed down. There are also white and bright red fruited forms. *Euonymus alatus* is a slow-growing plant eventually 6 foot high (1.8 m) and wide which develops strange corky 'wings' on its branches. The fruits – purplish with scarlet seeds – are not freely produced; its chief glory lies in the brilliant rosy scarlet autumn foliage.

Stranvaesia davidiana var. *undulata* is reminiscent of a cotoneaster and its dark green evergreen leaves are brightly tinted in spring and have the unusual habit of causing their oldest leaves to turn red, contrasting pleasantly with the younger green ones. The coloured leaves drop before winter. It is grown for the brilliant coral-red fruits which are carried in pendant bunches all along the branches. The fact that they seem bird-proof adds to its value. There is a yellow-fruited form *S. davidiana* 'Fructu Luteo'.

The North American snowberry takes its common name from its profusion of snow-white berries whose weight causes its branches to arch over gracefully in the autumn and winter throughout which they persist.

It is *Symphoricarpos rivularis*, which is one of the parents of that excellent hybrid *S.* × *doorenbosii*. This has pinkish berries and is superseded by some of the clones to which it has given rise. *S. d.* 'Erectum' makes a good small hedge bearing rosy lilac berries if not too hard clipped; 'Magic Berry' is compact and pink berried. 'Mother of Pearl' is particularly fine, a small dense shrub bearing an immense crop of rosy flushed white fruits.

Leycesteria formosa would not, I suppose, be in everyone's list of best shrubs, but to me the sea-green hollow cane-like stems are so unusual and attractive in winter and the tiny white flowers hanging in 6 inch long panicles (15 cm) surrounded by conspic-uous claret-coloured bracts so different that it is well worth finding a place for, even if it did not have the intriguing common name of grandmother's curls, which indeed it does resemble, especially in autumn when shining purple-red berries replace the flowers. These in turn give rise to another of its common names, the pheasant berry, that bird being said to be very partial to them.

Climbers, Scramblers and Wall Plants

Climbing plants may support themselves in many different ways – by aerial roots, by twining, by hooked thorns, or by clasping with leaf tendrils. The importance of this to the gardener is that he should observe each plant's method of growth, and then do his best to provide the most appropriate kind of support (e.g. trellis or wires).

Remarkably few climbers which are really garden-worthy are able to cling without help to a wall or fence. Among them are natural varieties of the common ivy, *Hedera helix*, and the Persian ivy, *H. colchica* 'Dentata Variegata', in whose leaves gold and green and cream are overlaid so attractively. All these cling limpet-like by aerial roots. The climbing hydrangea, *Hydrangea anomala* ssp. *petiolaris*, a magnificent creamy white flowered shrub in full spate in July, is also self-clinging (see p. 11).

The best known clingers are the Virginia creeper, *Parthenocissus quinquefolia* and its relative, the Boston ivy, *P. tricuspidata* 'Veitchii', both clothing walls with splendid autumnal scarlet.

The scramblers or smotherers are much more numerous. One of the familiar sights of chalkland hedges is the spectacle of *Clematis vitalba*, or old man's beard, climbing as high as it can get up thorn or other small trees and cascading down on the lightest side in its curtains of greenish flowers which in autumn turn to that glistening foam of seed heads which gives rise to its common name. Some of its relatives like *C. montana*, or *C. armandii*, will grow in the same fashion, smothering any plant in their way (see p. 11). Marvellous though they are in the right setting, beware and do not plant near anything you treasure. Of course there are many charming clematis which are not so overbearing, *C. macropetala*, for example, whose nodding violet-blue lantern-shaped flowers appear in May. They never look better than when clambering by means of their petioles through a slender shrub like a mock orange and they usually tolerate each other to the advantage of all.

The large-flowered clematis are among the most popular and spectacular of garden plants. Most are best placed on walls as they may overweigh the light shrubs you may wish to grow them through. It is wise, therefore, to choose the less vigorous. More details of these appear on p. 54.

The striking autumn tints of *Parthenocissus tricuspidata* 'Veitchii'

In the wild too you may see a honeysuckle, *Lonicera periclyme-num*, twining its stems in iron hard bands around anything it can reach. Some cultivated types will do the same in the garden. Let this emphasise that scramblers are fierce colonisers of every available space. You can use this to advantage. A shady place under trees where little will grow can be colonised by the Irish ivy, *Hedera helix* 'Hibernica'. Once established it is a most pleasant glossy green, is completely weed-proof and rarely tries to climb the trees. In a more sunny place honeysuckles can be most effective, notably *Lonicera acuminata* or the late Dutch, *L.* 'Serotina'.

When planting a shrub to climb a bush or tree, make a planting hole some distance, at least 3 feet (90 cm) from the host plant. Train the leading shoot along the ground and tie into place on the host; this reduces competition for water and food.

PLANTING ON WALLS

Most of us have walls to deal with either on the house or boundaries. Before selecting suitable plants it is wise to make sure that the conditions will allow them to grow, for all too often builders find it convenient to leave their rubble there covered with a skin of soil and there may well be a projecting concrete footing. With the latter you can do nothing but make your planting arrangements beyond it; as for rubble, it has to be dug out to a depth and width of 2 feet (60 cm) and replaced with good soil. An exhausting chore, but one whose reward is spread over many years as your plants grow and thrive.

A south-facing wall is the easiest to deal with, being the warmest, followed by west, then east and lastly north; but all have plants well suited to them. Often plants of doubtful hardiness in your district can be grown against a wall where there is shelter from winds and the absorbed heat of bricks, etc., gives night protection. There are snags in that one of the ways in which flowers can be destroyed is for them to be exposed to an early burst of sun following a sharp night frost. This causes a rapid expansion rupturing the cell walls. Most of the victims are likely to be those on the walls first warmed by the morning sun, i.e. the south and east walls. The danger months are March and April so plant shrubs which flower at this period on the west or north facing walls.

North walls are commonly regarded as being difficult sites for growing plants. It may need more thought but there is quite a long list of suitable plants whose beauty and interest can capture the attention. (See also the Wisley handbook, *Plants for Shade.*)

The principles to guide one in choosing for all walls are that one should intersperse climbers which need to be spread out and tied to the wall with shrubs which are happy to grow against the protective face largely unsupported, such as *Ceanothus*. Include also some which are distinctive by reason of their golden or silver variegation or by their leaf shape alone. Flowering times, too, should span the year as much as possible.

It is a common belief – which has little to support it – that climbers, especially the self-clinging kinds like some ivies, damage the walls on which they grow. Of course commonsense is needed; it would obviously be unwise to plant climbers on a wall

Clematis 'Nelly Moser', a good plant for a shady wall

in need of pointing or up a plastered structure in which there were cracks which could be enlarged by root invasion, but otherwise structural damage is unlikely. It is important to prevent climbers from spreading into gutters and under tiles where they can cause serious damage. Once they have reached that height a yearly cut back *before* they start to grow is advisable.

Wall supports are generally necessary. The oldest method, and still the best, is to have the wall wired at about 1½ feet (45 cm) spacing. You can put in nails as required but many walls have such hard mortar that wall nails bend – to drill and plug each nail is demanding of both time and temper.

More expensive alternatives are wooden or metal trellis. The latter are often plastic-covered, the colour, especially the greens, leaves much to be desired. Black or dark brown are rarely objectionable.

North and east walls

Celastrus orbiculatus	Yellow and orange fruited climber.
Chaenomeles – Any	Japanese quince, "Japonica".
Clematis montana var. *rubens*	Pink, Prolific. May-flowering. Vigorous.
Clematis 'Nelly Moser' *Clematis* 'Comtesse de Bouchaud'	Pale colours which do not bleach on this wall (see p. 53).
Clematis orientalis	Called 'orange peel' clematis because of its thick sepals.
Choisya ternata	Mexican orange blossom. White. May. Fragrant.
Euonymus fortunei and cvs.	Variegated and coloured leaves.
Garrya elliptica	Suede-grey catkins. March.
Hedera colchica and cvs.	Persian ivy. Handsome variegation.
Hedera helix cvs.	Many interesting variants of common ivy.
Hydrangea anomala ssp. *petiolaris*	Climbing hydrangea. White "flowers".
Jasminum nudiflorum	Cheerful in midwinter. Yellow flowers.
Kerria japonica 'Pleniflora'	Bright green stems. Yellow, double flowers. April (see p. 39).
Lonicera tragophylla	Bright yellow. Summer.
Mahonia japonica	Winter, Yellow. Lily-of-the-valley scented.
Pyracantha – Any	Bright autumn fruits.

South and west walls

Abelia floribunda	Red. June. Tender.
Abutilon megapotamicum	Lantern-shaped red flowers. May.
Acacia dealbata	Mimosa.
Campsis radicans	Trumpet vine. Orange/red.
Ceanothus spp.	One of the bluest of shrubs.
Chimonanthus praecox	Wintersweet. January.
Clematis cvs.	Need a cool root run.
Cytisus battandieri	Moroccan broom. Pineapple-scented.

Fremontodendron californicum	Bright golden cups. Summer.
Lippia citriodora	Lemon scented foliage.
Magnolia grandiflora	Large walls only. White goblets.
Passiflora caerulea	Passion flower.
Phygelius capensis	Scarlet 'hunting horn' flowers in July.
Solanum crispum 'Glasnevin'	Purple-blue 'potato' flowers. Summer.
Wisteria sinensis	Lilac flowers. May/June.

Pyracantha coccinea 'Lalandei', *Hedera helix* 'Goldheart' and *Garrya elliptica*

Hedges

Choosing a hedging plant to succeed on a limy soil should present no problem on that score for no commonly used hedging plant refuses to grow in alkaline conditions.

Clarity of thought, however, is certainly needed before a choice is finally made. Some of the points at issue are what is the hedge for – to divide the garden? To provide privacy from neighbours? Is it to be decorative, i.e. bear flowers? Must it be evergreen or will deciduous do? Have you room on the boundary for the 5 feet (1.5 m) minimum necessary for a formal hedge, or would it be best to have a fence? How tall should it grow?

The answers to these problems are specific to the garden and its owner. Some of the most satisfactory choices are indicated below.

All the best tall hedges are slow growing but well worth waiting for. The yew, *Taxus baccata*, is a native tree commonly found on chalk or limestone. It makes the handsomest of all hedges and has a reputation for extreme slowness which is not merited. Apart from our excellent native, the hybrid between it and *T. cuspidata*, the Japanese yew – *Taxus × media*, has given rise to two very good hedging cultivars known as 'Hatfieldii' and 'Hicksii'.

The western red cedar, *Thuya plicata*, has much to commend it. Even on thin chalk it makes a splendid bright green hedge. It needs to be trimmed for shape and density in August. A pleasant job, for when handled it gives off an attractive scent; some say it reminds them of pineapple (see opposite).

Holly is another superb hedger. Of its many forms the best may be *Ilex × altaclerensis*, the Highclere holly. Its leaves are almost thornless, which makes life easier when weeding near it. It has many variants from which 'Jermyns', with leaves of plain polished green and 'Lawsoniana', which has an attractive golden variegation, can be chosen with confidence.

Still among the tall evergreen hedges there are circumstances when speed of growth is the most important consideration. Fastest growing of all is the Leyland cypress, *× Cupressocyparis leylandii*, commonly adding 2 feet (60 cm) or more to its height each year. Since they can be planted 2½ feet apart (75 cm), it is also a cheap hedge. The rapid rate of growth makes it imperative that the ground rules for the trimming of all newly-planted conifer hedges are followed. Allow the plants to settle down for a year and as soon as normal growth starts trim the terminal growths

The Welsh poppy, *Meconopsis cambrica*, under a yew hedge

with secateurs. This will encourage the dense solid basal growth so prized in later years. Lawson's cypress, *Chamaecyparis lawsoniana* also makes a good hedge and its cultivar 'Green Hedger' is widely used. Vegetatively raised plants must be used if a hedge of even growth and colour is desired.

Among the tall deciduous hedges beech, *Fagus sylvatica*, and hornbeam, *Carpinus betulus*, are the most widely acclaimed. Grown as hedges, they are hard to distinguish save that the former has a smooth leaf edge and the latter is serrated. Clipped in July, there is time for short growths to develop before autumn and the leaves they bear after turning a delightful golden brown will stay on all winter. An additional character can be given to such hedges by including a few purple or copper beech seedlings when planting at random spacing. The famous 'tapestry' hedge at Hidcote Manor, Gloucestershire is a good example.

Privet and hawthorn (or quick) need considering as they are cheap and effective if well maintained. Even so, privet disqualifies itself for many as it requires clipping three or even four times a year to look well and it robs a considerable area of nearby soil of nutrients by its exuberant root system. Thorn hedges may be dull to look at compared with those mentioned above, but they have many virtues apart from cheapness. They are so dense that you cannot see through them even in mid-winter; the young growth in spring is a pleasant pink and it needs but one clip a year at mid-summer. It is also the favourite hedge of our smaller native birds – perhaps a two-edged virtue.

INFORMAL HEDGES

These are not clipped, but grown for their flower or berry. The taller kinds need double the width of a formal hedge – around 10 feet (2.1 m) – to develop properly.

Berberis × stenophylla, apart from being one of the finest of all evergreen shrubs, is perhaps the most widely planted for hedging. It forms a dense hedge up to 10 feet high (2.1 cm) from which it throws slender arching sprays of narrow dark green leaves. In April the sprays are bowed down in a myriad of tiny golden flowers. Prune by secateurs immediately these go over to encourage young growths to flower the following spring. For smaller spaces two excellent but less vigorous forms are 'Irwinii' and 'Coccinea' with deep yellow and crimson buds respectively. Container grown plants are advisable.

One of the parents of the above hybrid is B. darwinii, which is of a stiffer habit; it bears small holly-like leaves and a rich profusion of orange-yellow blooms in the spring. These are usually followed by an attractive display of plum-coloured berries in the autumn.

Among the hedges for dividing garden areas or beside paths, lavender is a universal favourite, especially on chalk. Of many clones, Lavandula angustifolia 'Vera' is the largest, 3 feet (90 cm) or more high and even more across. This is Dutch lavender, the commercial source of oil of lavender. A better, more compact garden plant is L. angustifolia 'Hidcote' about half the size of 'Vera', bearing abundant violet-blue flowers in July. Clip over with shears immediately after flowering for compact growth.

There are a number of non-flowering honeysuckles offered as hedging plants. Most common is that known in the trade as Nitida, Lonicera nitida 'Ernest Wilson', but much better in that it is less liable to damage by snow, dogs, children or for that matter neglect of clipping, is 'Yunnan'. This is stouter, more erect in habit and can be clipped into an attractive durable hedge.

One of the most useful and attractive shrubs for the garden is Berberis thunbergii, invaluable for yellow spring flowers, brilliant red/orange autumn foliage and deep red berries. It will make a hedge about a yard wide and as much high as a low garden division. Better where there is less room is B. Thunbergii 'Erecta'. It is half as wide but may be 4 foot high (1.2 m).

PLANTING HEDGES

Traditionally hedging plants are set out as a staggered double row. This is demanding on food reserves in the soil and costly, as many more plants are needed than the single row now usually used. Single rows can look disappointingly thin when first planted but the spaces soon fill up with healthy growth. Especially on chalk or limestone the site for the hedge should be well broken up to 18 inches deep (45 cm) and humus liberally added. Buy plants which are bushy and short-jointed with fibrous root systems. Firm moist roots indicate a healthy plant capable of rapid growth. Plants should be as similar as possible to ensure even growth and appearance throughout the length of the hedge.

Deciduous hedges should be planted between October and March when they are dormant. Evergreens are best planted as near the end of April as possible.

Take out the trench about 2 feet wide (60 cm) on the prepared ground, fork in 4 oz (113 g) coarse bone meal per yard (90 cm) run into the base. Place the shrub in the centre spreading out the roots and cover with fine soil. Then fill in the rest of the soil, firming well with the heel as you go. Make sure the shrubs are at the same soil level as when they were growing in the nursery; this is easily seen by the 'tide-mark' left by the nursery soil on the stems. Water well in dry weather.

Distance apart may vary from 1 foot (30 cm) to 4 feet (1.2 m) according to the size of the species at maturity.

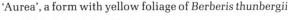

'Aurea', a form with yellow foliage of *Berberis thunbergii*

Ground Cover and Bulbs

Weeding is one of the most time-consuming and tiresome of the garden's tasks. Ground cover is a simple idea designed to make life easier for the busy gardener.

Nature thought up the idea long before Man needed it; a clump of impenetrable gorse, a nettle bed or a heather-clad moor, are all cases where a single plant has achieved such root dominance that other plants are excluded. If you have a well-established bed of lily-of-the-valley in your garden you will be familiar with the same kind of total dominance of one species.

We introduce ground cover into our gardens primarily to suppress weeds, but it also deals with that dry spot under trees, with awkward banks, with spaces in front of shrub plantings or where annual plantings are inconvenient.

It does have disadvantages. For a year or two it is labour-intensive as the plants must be kept weed-free until they touch and intertwine, and it may be expensive to buy the plants. However, it is a real investment, not only in time eventually, but also in money if labour has to be paid.

When weeding keep a sharp look out for young brambles and tree seedlings, especially ash and sycamore; if allowed to root deeply they are difficult to remove. Once established ground cover provides a perfect natural economy. The leaves prevent excessive baking by the sun; the roots prevent soil-scouring in heavy rain and the leaf fall a natural feeding mulch.

It is unfortunate that so many excellent carpeters are lime-hating – the heathers largely, *Gaultheria*, and so on, but there is still a wide selection. (For further ideas on ground cover see the handbook of that title published in this series).

Among the heathers all the winter-flowering family of *Erica carnea* are suitable and it is a prolific one – at least two dozen cultivars ranging from 'Springwood White' to the deep red 'Ruby Glow'. They are quite happy in all alkaline soils save the thinnest of chalks.

To give a little height you can introduce *E. erigena*, which is deep pink and up to a yard tall (90 cm) or the hybrid between these two, *E.* × *darleyensis*, about $1\frac{1}{2}$ feet (45 cm) and rose pink. The Corsican heath *E. terminalis* is a pink 2-foot (60 cm) summer-flowering lime lover. Junipers are natural plants of the chalk and associate well with heathers.

Euphorbia robbiae provides good ground cover

The best low-growing drybank shrub is the rose of Sharon, *Hypericum calycinum*. It loves the sun and produces far more of its golden cups in summer here than in shade, but it will grow and grow well even there. Keep well cut back each February with shears. Do not blame it if in a few years it proves to have a will of its own and tries to take over more than its allotted space. The same applies to that excellent shade plant *Euphorbia robbiae*. It is an evergreen spurge, dark green with a cloud of pale green inflorescences in the spring, most useful to flower arrangers.

Equally able to cope with shade are the periwinkles, *Vinca major* and *V. minor*, though they flower better in a sunny spot. I prefer the latter, it is closer growing and roots more readily at the nodes as the shoots run along. Clip them over in March and you will see the flowers much better.

Lonicera pileata is a semi-evergreen with small dark green leaves and horizontal branches. It grows equally successfully in dry conditions and in the full sun and is a neglected plant for this purpose. *Mahonia aquifolium*, the Oregon grape, can be used in the same way.

Among the non-shrubby ground coverers is the variegated yellow archangel *Lamium galeobdolon* 'Variegatum'. Its evergreen foliage is pleasantly marbled with silver. Its unremarkable yellow flowers appear as spikes in spring. Very rampant, it is one of the most useful ground-cover plants under trees. Its relative, *L. maculatum* is more amenable to discipline, making an evergreen mat, each purplish leaf of which has a central white flash. The flowers according to cultivar are white, magenta or pink. *Bergenia cordifolia*, with its huge 'elephants ears' as leaves, is not only one of the finest suppressors of weeds, but most valuable as a foliage contrast. I have already referred to lily of the valley, *Convallaria majalis*. Surely no plant pays a higher dividend – incomparable scent, pleasant unusual flowers and ruthless suppression of all competition when it likes its home.

BULBS

Lilies are the only bulbs which show a marked dislike of alkaline soils. The species involved are mainly from North America and Japan (see p. 22).

A great many new hybrids have been produced in North America and Canada. Sometimes one of the calcifuges has been used as a parent; this characteristic is sometimes passed on, sometimes not, so it is wise to regard all these most beautiful hybrids with suspicion unless categorically recommended for limy soils. Unfortunately some catalogues do not make this clear. Many of these hybrids are short-lived even in soils which suit them. This habit is likely to be accentuated on chalky soils so approach them with caution or consider growing them in pots.

All this caution should not obscure the fact that many lilies do very well on alkaline soils, for example *L. candidum, L. regale, L. × testaceum* and indeed all the European lilies. It is a very wide selection, but you do need to study and obey their quite simple needs.

Few other bulbs have such demands but they have a common need, most especially on chalk, for food. Most bulbs, like daffodils on good soils, once properly planted need little attention. On light alkaline soils, however, annual feeding is a necessity. Mulch with a good compost or apply a complete fertilizer (such as Growmore) at 2–3 oz per square yard (66 to 100 g/m²). Apply this before the bulbs' roots start to grow, i.e. in the case of daffodils from summer to October.

Vegetables

There are no vegetables which refuse to grow because of their dislike of lime. Indeed, the whole of the cabbage family are the better for it in that they are less subject to club root disease. However, good vegetables will not be produced if there is lack of water and this can be avoided by adding ample supplies of moisture-retaining humus by some of the methods outlined earlier (see pages 18–21). Do remember that the influence of peat, etc., is shortlived. It is rare to find any trace a year later on chalky land. Potatoes are more than usually subject to scab. This organism lives on the dead skin, not on the edible parts which remain sound, but does make an unpleasant disfiguration. Root vegetables are often advised against on chalky soils but are not a serious problem except to those wanting to show exhibition vegetables. Stump-rooted carrots are perfectly satisfactory for domestic purposes, for example. Parsnips are inclined to fork and it may be worth resorting to the old trick of boring a hole with a dibber the size of root you hope for and filling it with sieved soil or potting soil. Sow a few seeds on each site, so that thinning is a minor job. This will be a benefit for large carrots as the smell of carrot caused by thinning is a magnet for the dreaded carrot fly. Turnips and globe beetroot are no problem. Swedes can be mildew-attacked on dry sites and are best sown late – in June – which avoids much trouble. If there were any vegetable I would advise against, it might be celery. It really does need a deep rich consistently moist soil. Choose cabbage lettuce rather than the moisture-loving cos types.

Overall, remember there is likely to be a shortage of potash. Frequent small applications of sulphate of potash should be given, to the root crops especially. Encouragement to leafy growth by light dressings of sulphate of ammonia is most rewarding.

Index

Page numbers in **bold** refer to illustrations